Fact Finders®

The Story of the
Civil War

The BIGGEST BATTLES of the CIVIL WAR

by Molly Kolpin

CAPSTONE PRESS
a capstone imprint

Fact Finders Books are published by Capstone Press,
1710 Roe Crest Drive, North Mankato, Minnesota 56003
www.capstonepub.com

Copyright © 2015 by Capstone Press, a Capstone imprint. All rights reserved. No part of this publication may be reproduced in whole or in part, or stored in a retrieval system, or transmitted in any form or by any means, electronic, mechanical, photocopying, recording, or otherwise, without written permission of the publisher.

Library of Congress Cataloging-in-Publication Data
Kolpin, Molly.
 The biggest battles of the Civil War / by Molly Kolpin.
    pages cm. — (Fact finders. The story of the Civil War)
 Includes bibliographical references and index.
 Summary: "Describes the biggest battles of the American Civil War, including the first and second Battles of Bull Run, Gettysburg, Antietam, and Shiloh"— Provided by publisher.
  ISBN 978-1-4914-0718-9 (library binding)
  ISBN 978-1-4914-0725-7 (pbk.)
  ISBN 978-1-4914-0729-5 (ebook pdf)
 1. United States—History—Civil War, 1861-1865—Campaigns—Juvenile literature. I. Title.
 E470.K63 2014
 973.7'3—dc23   2014007636

Developed and Produced by Focus Strategic Communications, Inc.
 Adrianna Edwards: project manager
 Ron Edwards, Jessica Pegis: editors
 Rob Scanlan: designer and compositor
 Karen Hunter: media researcher
 Francine Geraci: copyeditor and proofreader
 Wendy Scavuzzo: fact checker

Photo Credits
Corbis, 6, 26, adoc-photos, 5, Bettmann, 25, Francis G. Mayer, 11; Library of Congress: Prints and Photographs Division, 9, 10, 13, 15, 18, 19, 21, 23; North Wind Picture Archives, 7, 17; Shutterstock: Christophe Boisson, stars and stripes design, vectorbomb, cover exploding bomb

Printed in the United States of America.
001159

Table of Contents

Chapter 1	A Conflicted Country	4
Chapter 2	Let the Battles Begin	6
Chapter 3	The North Scores	20
Chapter 4	The South Surrenders	24

Glossary	30
Read More	31
Critical Thinking Using the Common Core	31
Internet Sites	32
Index	32

A Conflicted Country

It was the mid-1800s in the United States. The North and South were at a standoff. The states could not agree on the issue of slavery. Northern states wanted slavery to be abolished. Southern states wanted to keep slavery.

In the North most people viewed slavery as cruel. Black men and women had been shipped to the United States against their will. They were forced into slavery. They did backbreaking work on large Southern plantations. Many were abused by their owners.

In the South feelings about slavery weren't so simple. Plantation owners needed slaves to help with their farms. Without slave labor, they couldn't make much money. The Southern way of life would collapse. This fear was so great that 11 Southern states decided to secede from the United States. These states wanted to form their own country. They also wanted to make their own laws.

abolish: to put an end to something officially

plantation: a large farm found in warm areas; before the Civil War, plantations in the South used slave labor

secede: to withdraw formally from a group or an organization, often to form another organization

The Northern states, however, weren't ready to part from the South. They wanted the country to remain united. Both sides were prepared to fight for what they believed in. By April 1861 the U.S. Civil War (1861-1865) had begun.

African-American men and women worked on plantations, like this one in South Carolina.

North vs. South: A Guide to Both Sides

	North	South
Political Names	the Union	Confederate States of America (also known as the Confederacy)
Nicknames	Yankees	Rebels
Uniform Colors	blue	gray
Presidents	Abraham Lincoln	Jefferson Davis
Capitals	Washington, D.C.	Richmond, Virginia
Main Army Names	Army of the Potomac	Army of Northern Virginia

Let the Battles Begin

Battle of Fort Sumter

South Carolina was the first Southern state to leave the United States. After breaking away, it took control of any federal property within its borders. One such property was Fort Sumter. It was located near Charleston Harbor.

The Confederates told Union troops to abandon Fort Sumter on April 11, 1861. But the Union would not give in. When Confederate troops fired on April 12, the Union fired back. Soon the Union was nearly out of food and ammunition.

After just one day of fighting, they surrendered to the Confederates. Only one soldier died in the battle. But the fighting started a long and deadly war, with many more battles to come.

Confederate troops fired cannon balls on Fort Sumter.

ammunition: bullets and other objects that can be fired from weapons

surrender: to give up or admit defeat

The Reality of War

Although the Civil War was bloody, people often watched the action from the battlefield sidelines or rooftops.

When the Civil War started, most Americans believed it would be over quickly. They had no idea the fighting would continue for four long years. They also did not understand the horrors of war. In the early days, they sometimes treated battles like a sport. They gathered on the sidelines to watch the fighting.

It wasn't long before people realized that the Civil War was a brutal conflict. Many lives were lost, and families were torn apart.

First Battle of Bull Run

In July 1861 Union General Irvin McDowell had a plan. He wanted control of a railroad in the Southern town of Manassas, Virginia. He decided to invade the town. With a railroad, he could transport Union soldiers and supplies whenever he needed.

Unknown to McDowell, Confederate General P. G. T. Beauregard had spies in Washington. He found out about McDowell's plan. He stationed 21,000 troops near a creek called Bull Run. This was bad news for the Union. To get to Manassas, they would have to pass both a creek and an army.

The battle began on July 21. At first the 35,000 Union soldiers successfully pushed back the Confederates. But then Confederate General Thomas "Stonewall" Jackson had an idea. He ordered the Confederate soldiers to stand like a stone wall. The Union troops would have to come to them.

The plan worked. The wall of soldiers slowed down the Union troops. After Confederate reinforcements arrived, the Rebels made one final charge. The Union soldiers fled. The Confederacy won again.

reinforcements: an additional supply of soldiers

The Confederacy won the First Battle of Bull Run.

FAST FACTS Many Civil War battles have more than one name. Northern states named battles after the nearest river or stream. Southern states named battles after the nearest town. The First Battle of Bull Run is also called the First Battle of Manassas.

Battle of Shiloh

In 1862 the Union wanted control of more transportation. This time they wanted a waterway instead of a railroad. Union General Ulysses S. Grant stationed an army at Shiloh along the Tennessee River. There he planned to wait for a second Union army to arrive from Nashville.

But things didn't go according to plan. Confederate General Albert Sidney Johnston wanted to attack the Union before their reinforcements arrived. On the morning of April 6, he ordered his Confederate soldiers to charge.

Union General Ulysses S. Grant

The Union troops were shocked. Thousands of Confederate troops were invading their camp. They had to start fighting with no warning. In an area called the Hornet's Nest, the violence was intense. Soon the Union troops had to surrender.

Luckily, more Union troops arrived just in time. The fresh group of Union soldiers attacked the Confederates. On April 7 the Confederates retreated. Victory went to the Union, but it came at a high price. When the fighting ended, nearly 24,000 Union and Confederate soldiers were dead, wounded, or missing.

Both Sides of the Story

One month before the Battle of Shiloh, there was another important battle. It was known as the Battle of the Ironclads. Ironclads were ships made of iron. Before this time, warships had always been made of wood.

The Confederacy ship was the CSS *Virginia*. The Union ship was the USS *Monitor*. The two ships came face to face on March 9, 1862. They fired cannons at one another. But both ships' iron plates protected them from harm.

The battle ended in a tie. However, the battle changed warfare on water. After this battle, wooden ships were never used again.

The CSS *Virginia* (left) and the USS *Monitor* (right) clashed at sea. Iron ships were ugly but well protected.

Second Battle of Bull Run

The Second Battle of Bull Run took place in August 1862. Union General John Pope and his troops waited at a bridge crossing at the upper Rappahannock River. Pope planned to attack the Confederates as soon as more troops arrived.

With the Union troops in a secure position, Confederate General Robert E. Lee had to think fast. He boldly split his army in two. Half of the soldiers were sent to march up behind Pope's troops. When Union soldiers saw the Confederates, they jumped into action. Though their reinforcements had not yet arrived, they fought well.

The Union soldiers, however, had no idea they were fighting only half the Confederate army. One day later the second half of the Confederate troops approached from the opposite direction. The surprised Union soldiers had no time to prepare. They lost to the Confederates at Bull Run once again.

During the Second Battle of Bull Run, Union forces attacked the Confederates. But the Union lost the battle when Confederates attacked from a different direction.

Battle of Antietam

In 1862 General Lee decided to enter enemy territory. He placed an army on the west side of Antietam Creek in Sharpsburg, Maryland. On the east side of Antietam Creek, Union General George B. McClellan set up his own army.

Fighting broke out on September 17. The Union soldiers repeatedly charged at the Confederates. But the Confederates kept pushing them back. In a sunken road at the center of the front lines, the fighting was bloody. This area came to be known as Bloody Lane.

Eventually, Union soldiers succeeded in pushing Confederate troops away from a stone bridge. The Union soldiers charged across the bridge. They entered the west side of Antietam Creek. But just then, Confederate reinforcements arrived. The armies fought until nightfall when the Confederates finally retreated. The Union had won the battle, but more than 23,000 Union and Confederate soldiers were dead, wounded, or missing.

Union soldiers charged across a bridge toward Antietam Creek during the Battle of Antietam.

FAST FACTS

Lee wrote his plans for the Battle of Antietam on paper. He did not know that a Union soldier found some of his notes on September 13. The Union used the notes to prepare for the fight. Some historians believe this may have helped them win the battle.

Battle of Fredericksburg

In late 1862 Union General Ambrose Burnside decided to target the Confederate capital of Richmond, Virginia. To get to Richmond, however, his army first had to pass through the city of Fredericksburg. Unfortunately, Fredericksburg was located on the opposite side of the Rappahannock River.

Burnside hoped to build a bridge and cross the river before General Lee could prepare the Confederates. But the Union's bridge supplies arrived late. This gave the Confederates plenty of time to set up for battle. They dug trenches in the hillsides. From there they fired at Union soldiers while staying protected.

On December 11 Union soldiers finally entered Fredericksburg. They took over the city without a problem. But two days later, they left Fredericksburg and entered an open field leading to Richmond. Surrounding the open field were the trenches dug by Confederate troops. When bullets started flying from the hillsides, Union troops knew they had lost. Soldiers were forced to retreat and let the Confederates claim another victory.

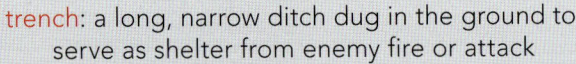

trench: a long, narrow ditch dug in the ground to serve as shelter from enemy fire or attack

The Battle of Fredericksburg was won by the Confederates, but it left the Southern city in ruins.

Battle of Chancellorsville

By 1863 the North knew of Robert E. Lee's brilliance as a general. He had led the Confederates to many victories. So when General Joseph Hooker became the new Union commander, he had a clear goal. He wanted to catch General Lee and his army.

Generals Stonewall Jackson (left) and Robert E. Lee are shown together in 1863.

On April 30 Hooker's troops began to march toward Lee's men in Fredericksburg. As they approached the Rebel line, the Confederates suddenly opened fire. The surprised Union soldiers rushed back to Chancellorsville, Virginia.

General Lee now made his riskiest decision yet. He left 10,000 soldiers to guard Fredericksburg. The remaining troops he divided into two groups. The first group went with Lee to chase Hooker's army. The second group went with Stonewall Jackson to form a surprise attack.

Jackson's soldiers marched 12 miles (19 kilometers) through a thick forest to get around Hooker's men. As darkness fell Jackson's army stormed out of the woods. The shell-shocked Union troops fought for four grueling days. But once again, the Confederates achieved victory.

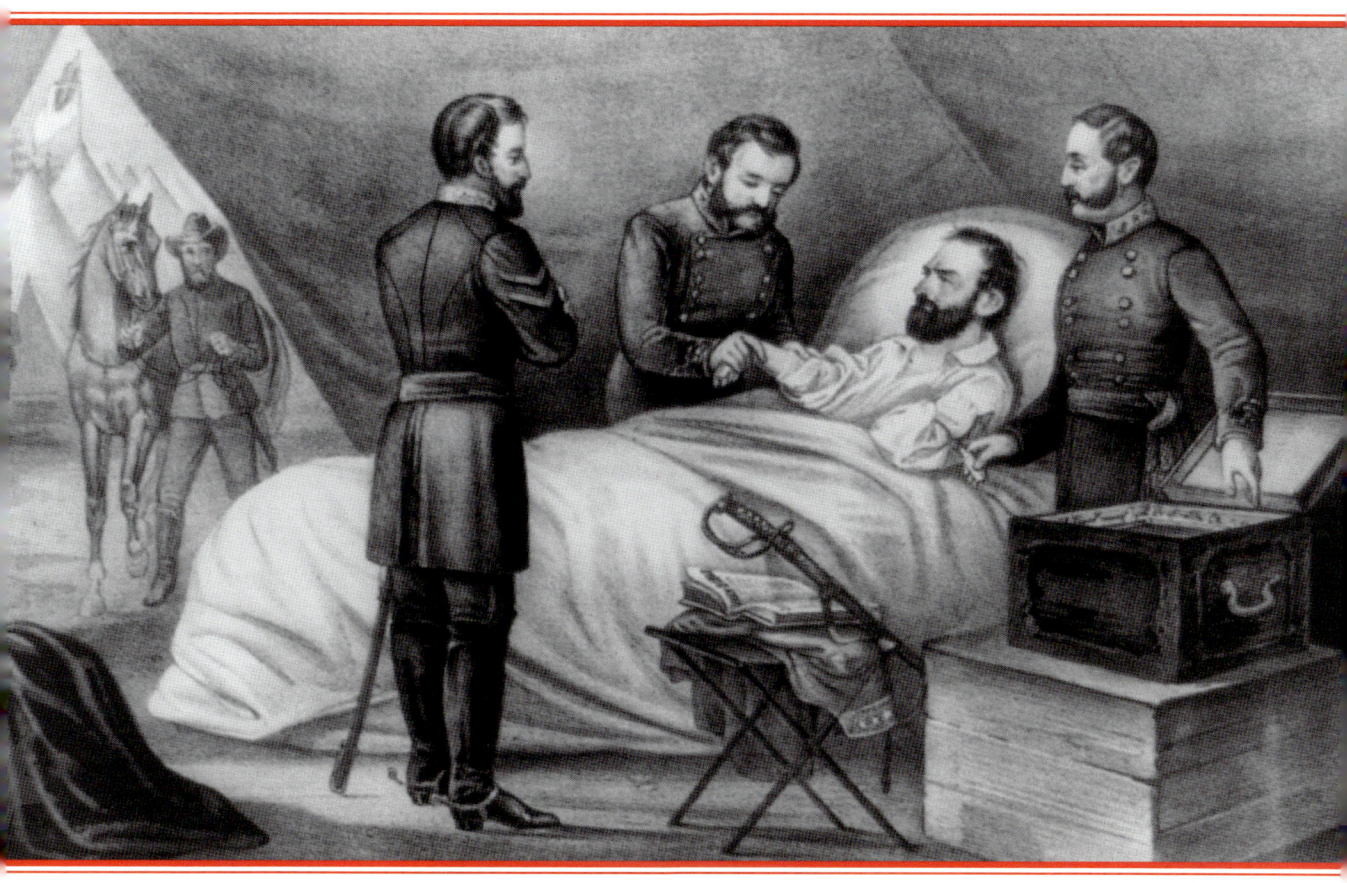

General Stonewall Jackson died after his left arm had to be amputated.

FAST FACTS

The Battle of Chancellorsville was a great win for the Confederates. But it also brought tragedy. During the fight, Stonewall Jackson was accidentally shot by his own soldiers. His left arm had to be **amputated**. While recovering, the celebrated Confederate general developed pneumonia and died.

amputate: to cut off someone's arm, leg, or other body part, usually because the part is damaged

The North Scores

Battle of Vicksburg

After their recent losses, the Union needed some good news. The South was gaining momentum—and the North was losing hope. Luckily, a major victory for the Union finally came in the summer of 1863.

Confederate troops in Vicksburg, Mississippi, took over a large section of the Mississippi River. They were able to transport men and supplies whenever they wished. President Abraham Lincoln believed the Union needed to capture Vicksburg in order to win the war.

For months, General Grant had been trying to attack Vicksburg from the north. Finally, he realized the key to victory was attacking from the south and east. Grant ordered his men to march south, where gunboats were able to ferry soldiers across the river.

Once on the eastern banks of the Mississippi River, Grant's men captured the capital city, Jackson. They then looped back west toward Vicksburg. They surrounded the city and attacked it from May 18 to July 4. Union gunboats on the river bombarded the area.

The city of Vicksburg was trapped on all sides. After a 47-day siege, the Confederates gave up. The Union had finally been able to take the city. They could now use the Mississippi River to transport Union troops and supplies.

During the battle, Union soldiers surrounded Vicksburg, Mississippi. Within 47 days they controlled the city.

siege: an attack designed to surround a place and cut it off from supplies or help

Battle of Gettysburg

The Union began to think it was on its way to winning the war. But the real turning point came with the Battle of Gettysburg. This three-day battle began on July 1, 1863, in Gettysburg, Pennsylvania.

On the first day of fighting, the Confederates drove the Union troops back into the hills. Day one ended with a Rebel victory. But the Rebels had made a mistake. Their opponents suddenly had the advantage of controlling higher ground.

The next day General George Meade stationed Union troops in a line across the top of a hill. The Confederates charged from their position at the hill's base. But the Union stopped them every time.

By day three Confederate General George Pickett arrived with reinforcements. In a desperate bid to win, about 12,000 Confederates marched toward the center of the Union line. This attack came to be called Pickett's Charge.

FAST FACTS

After the Battle of Gettysburg, part of the battlefield became a cemetery. During the cemetary's dedication, President Lincoln gave the Gettysburg Address. It opens with the famous line: "Four score and seven years ago our fathers brought forth on this continent, a new nation, conceived in liberty, and dedicated to the proposition that 'all men are created equal.'"

As the Confederates approached, both sides opened fire. Eventually, the enemies came face to face, fighting with their bayonets. But the Confederates were outnumbered. They retreated on July 4.

When the battle ended, more than 51,000 Union and Confederate soldiers had been killed, injured, or gone missing. The battle marked a turning point in the war. The Confederacy was unable to replace all the men and supplies it had lost. Finally, the end of the Civil War was in sight.

Battle of Gettysburg

bayonet: a long metal blade attached to the end of a musket or rifle

The South Surrenders

By late 1864 Grant knew a Union victory was near. His plan was to destroy the Confederates' supplies. Grant believed this would help end the war. He sent General William T. Sherman on a path of destruction now known as Sherman's March to the Sea.

Sherman and his men traveled to major cities across the South, including Atlanta, Savannah, Columbia, and Raleigh. They burned towns, ruined crops, destroyed property, and ripped up railroad tracks. They even reclaimed Fort Sumter—the federal property that was lost in the Civil War's first battle.

FAST FACTS

The fall of Atlanta was an especially hard blow to Southern pride. South Carolinian Mary Chestnut wrote in her diary, "Since Atlanta, I have felt as if ... we are going to be wiped off the earth."

Sherman's soldiers ripped up railway tracks on their march through the South.

Meanwhile, Grant's army chased the remaining Confederates to a small Virginia town called Appomattox Court House. There they surrounded the Rebels. On April 9, 1865, Lee surrendered. At long last the Civil War had come to an end.

The North and South fought 8,700 conflicts during the Civil War. About 750,000 people died. But when the war was over, the nation remained united. And that, perhaps, was the biggest Civil War victory of all.

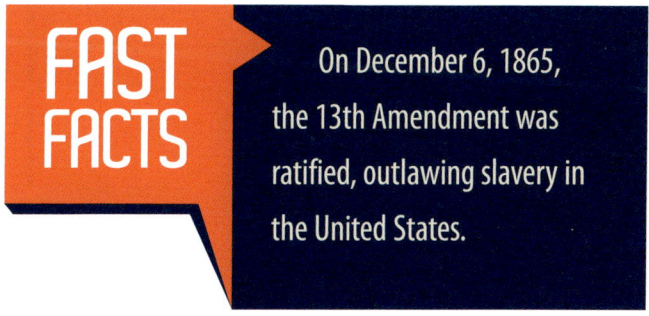

FAST FACTS: On December 6, 1865, the 13th Amendment was ratified, outlawing slavery in the United States.

Union General Ulysses S. Grant (left) and Confederate General Robert E. Lee (right) agreed to peace at the end of the Civil War.

Timeline of the Civil War's Biggest Battles

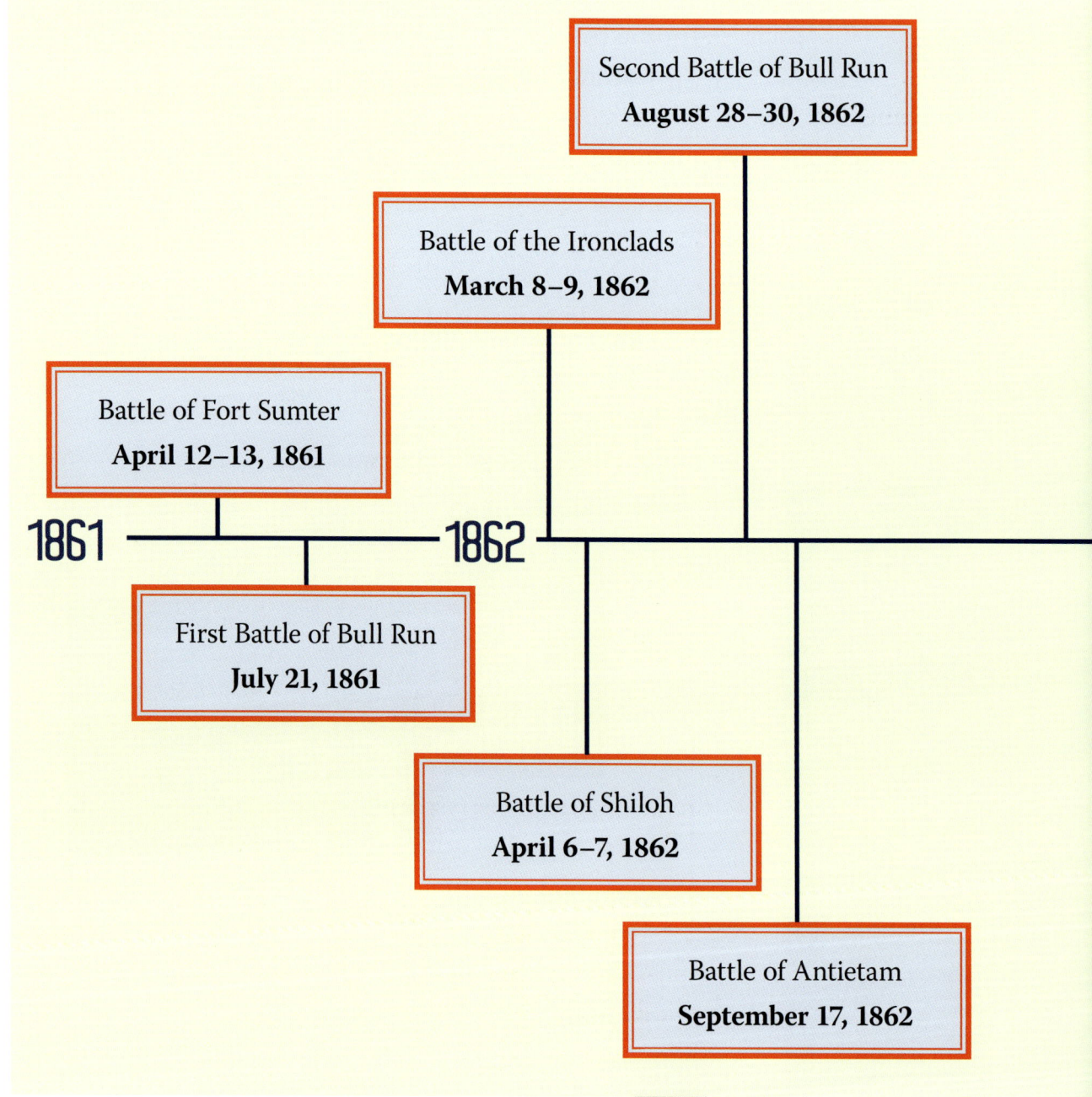

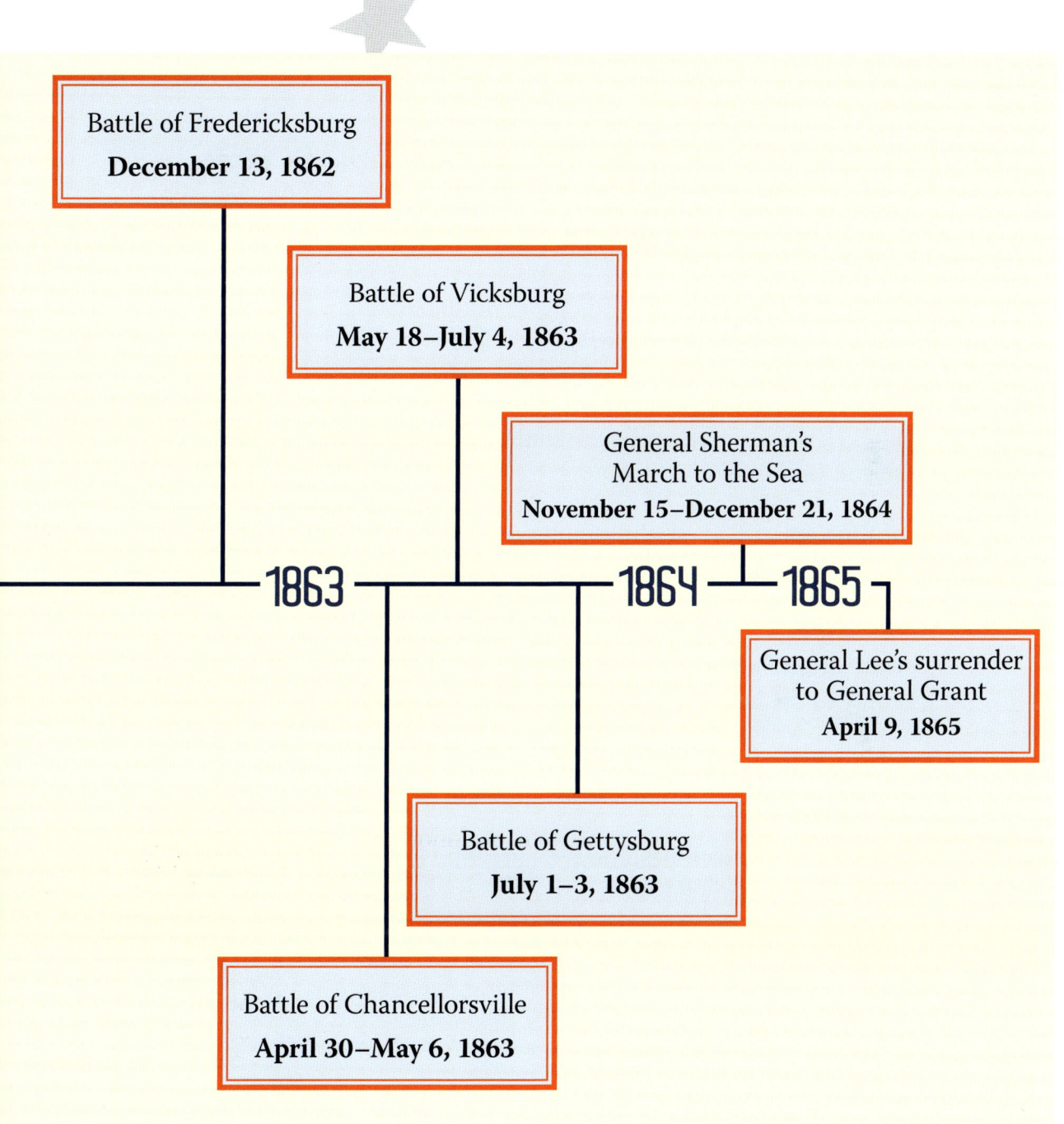

Glossary

abolish (uh-BOL-ish)—to put an end to something officially

ammunition (am-yuh-NI-shuhn)—bullets and other objects that can be fired from weapons

amputate (AM-pyuh-tayt)—to cut off someone's arm, leg, or other body part, usually because the part is damaged

bayonet (BEY-uh-net)—a long metal blade attached to the end of a musket or rifle

plantation (plan-TAY-shuhn)—a large farm found in warm areas; before the Civil War, plantations in the South used slave labor

reinforcements (ree-in-FORSS-muhnts)—an additional supply of soldiers

secede (si-SEED)—to withdraw formally from a group or an organization, often to form another organization

siege (seej)—an attack designed to surround a place and cut it off from supplies or help

surrender (suh-REN-dur)—to give up or admit defeat

trench (TRENCH)—a long, narrow ditch dug in the ground to serve as shelter from enemy fire or attack

Read More

Ollhoff, Jim. *The Civil War: Early Battles.* The Civil War. Minneapolis: ABDO Pub. Co., 2012.

Sandler, Martin W. *What Was America's Deadliest War? And Other Questions about the Civil War.* Good Question! New York: Sterling Children's Books, 2014.

Senzell Isaacs, Sally. *The Civil War.* All About America. New York: Kingfisher, 2011.

Critical Thinking Using the Common Core

1. What were two important battles of the Civil War? What evidence from the book supports your answer? (Key Ideas and Details)

2. On page 7 the author wrote: "It wasn't long before people realized that the Civil War was a brutal conflict." How do the illustrations in the book help to show this? Which illustration is the best proof of the author's point? Why? (Craft and Structure)

Internet Sites

FactHound offers a safe, fun way to find Internet sites related to this book. All of the sites on FactHound have been researched by our staff.

Here's all you do:

Visit www.facthound.com

Type in this code: 9781491407189

Check out projects, games, and lots more at www.capstonekids.com

Index

Antietam, Battle of, 14, 15, 28
Appomattox, 27, 29

Bull Run, First Battle of, 8, 9, 28
Bull Run, Second Battle of, 12–13, 28

Chancellorsville, Battle of, 18, 19, 29

Fort Sumter, Battle of, 6, 28
Fredericksburg, Battle of, 16–17, 29

Gettysburg Address, 22
Gettysburg, Battle of, 22–23, 29
Grant, Ulysses S., 10, 20, 24, 27, 29

Ironclads, Battle of the, 11, 28

Jackson, Thomas "Stonewall," 8, 18, 19

Lee, Robert E., 12, 14, 15, 16, 18, 26, 27, 29

Lincoln, Abraham, 20, 22, 23

Manassas, First Battle of, 9
March to the Sea (Sherman), 24, 25, 29
Monitor, USS (ironclad), 11

Sherman, William T., 24, 25, 29
Shiloh, Battle of, 10, 11, 28

Vicksburg, Battle of, 20–21, 29
Virginia, CSS (ironclad), 11